T0196722

LOOK OUT
THE
WINDOW

LOOK OUT
THE
WINDOW

PHYLLIS L WERNSING

LOOK OUT THE WINDOW

Cover Photo by Phyllis L. Wernsing
Photo taken at the Piedmont Environmental
Center in High Point, North Carolina

iUniverse books may be ordered through booksellers or by contacting:

iUniverse
1663 Liberty Drive
Bloomington, IN 47403
www.iuniverse.com
1-800-Authors (1-800-288-4677)

ISBN: 978-1-5320-3101-4 (sc)
ISBN: 978-1-5320-3102-1 (e)

Print information available on the last page.

iUniverse rev. date: 08/26/2017

This book is dedicated to the glory of God and to those who take time to see the beauty provided for them as they look out the windows of life.

Contents

Look Out The Window

I sat looking out the window where I often read my devotionals and write what is placed within my thinking. In the quietness of my prayer time I became aware of a thought that seemed to be speaking to me. Let me share that thought with you.

As I talked to the Lord, I heard myself saying: "Lord, I need to clean the window to my soul in order to see the beauty on the other side of my life. You know I cry within my being and fog seems to cover the Light placed before me. I know Your Light is within my reach, but it does not seem attainable this day. Forgive me. Amen."

I continued my time of thought and prayer. Please join me as I continue to place thoughts and feelings into my journal:

I feel that many times we do not recognize we are in the presence of God.

As we look out the window of our lives, we may gaze upon the beauty of a hummingbird hovering in the air as it gets nourishment from a flower… surely we are in the presence of God.

When we see the power of a river pushing through what lies before it… creating a great majestic waterfall… we are in the presence of God.

When a spring rain refreshes a thirsty garden… the presence of God is before us. When someone smiles… surely we are in the presence of God and when we pray… we **are** in the presence of God.

When we rest before God let us remember all He has done for us.

As I rest before God this day, I will be thankful for the blessing of sharing His gifts of thought, prayer and artistic expressions as I place within these pages two booklets of art. The first booklet is called "**The Beauty Within Each Season**." The other booklet is called "**Butterflies On The Wind**." I am also sharing some new thoughts for those who may have already read the booklets I have mentioned.

As you read this book, may the presence of God be with you as you become aware of His presence within your life. "**Look Out The Window**" and see all the beauty God has provided for us… even if you need to clean off the window to your soul in order to see it. Amen.

> *Psalm 43:5 RSV*
> *Why are you cast down, O my soul, and why are you disquieted within me? Hope in God; for I shall again praise him, my help and my God.*

Afraid To Travel

A friend was afraid to travel by herself. She would not come to visit us because she feared the unknown before her. "What if I should have car trouble along the way?" She asked. Her fear centered on some lonely roads she would need to travel to reach us. She depended on others to take her where she needed to go... especially if she needed to travel any distance from her home.

One day I suggested that she might try a well-traveled road. That way she can probably receive help if she should have a problem. Concern was in her eyes as she looked at me and quietly replied "Well, you cannot trust anyone these days." Although her statement was true, I had the feeling that nothing would be helpful. Nothing would allow her to feel better about her traveling arrangements.

As I thought about my friend, I realized that we often do the same thing in our daily lives. We do not like the lonely roads in life and we find fear with every turn... but we do not trust anyone on the busy highways either. We find ourselves trapped and restricted by our own fears.

Lord Jesus, Help us to trust in You as we travel on the roads that You have placed before us. If we should become lost or fearful, help us to take your hand and find comfort. By trusting in You, we will find our way. Amen.

Psalm 5:11 KJV

But let all those that put their trust in thee rejoice: let them ever shout for joy, because thou defendest them: let them also that love thy name be joyful in thee.

***

THOUGHTS FROM TIME TO TIME

I saw a picture of the Earth. I then saw a picture of a flower, a baby, a honey bee, a tree, small children playing in a playground, a group of people singing, horses in a pasture… the pictures went on and on. Finally, I heard a Friend say: Made with pride by God. Nothing else needed to be said.

***

Sorrow seemed to encompass my being. I looked upward and silently prayed: "Hold me close Lord…so I do not lose sight of Your face." Amen.

Guide Me Lord

Sometimes, to look forward, one must be willing to look back.

To confront that which haunts you.

To embrace it and cry.

Not alone, but with someone that can help you.

Sometimes caring may not be enough.

Many care.

Many people do not know what to say and are not able to handle your pain. But pain is real... In many ways, shapes and forms. Pain exists and all of us will experience it sometime in our lives.

Lord, I am searching for the one that can help me.

Hear my petition and grant me your guidance. I do not want to inflict pain on those that are unable to carry my pain for even a few moments.

And so, I seek guidance Lord.

I come to You in prayer.

I know that you will guide me. You will even **push** me, if necessary, in the direction that I need to go. I know that you will help me find the special beauty that life can give to me. Because in receiving, one can then give to those around them.

Thank you Lord for all that you do for me. Amen.

2 Corinthians 11:27 RSV

In toil and hardship, through many a sleepless night, in hunger and thirst, often without food, in cold and exposure. (I see that I am not alone Lord. There have been many in pain before me.)

Understand What You Read

I saw several people reading.

As they read the book before them, they began to daydream at the same time they were reading. I understood what was happening, but did not know why I saw what was placed within my thoughts. As I wondered about what I saw, a friend put down his book, smiled and said:

"It is possible to read and not perceive what you are reading. But when you do not perceive what you are reading you do not understand what you read."

Lord, forgive me for the times that I do not perceive what I read. Amen.

Exodus 24:7 RSV
Then he took the book of the covenant, and read it in the hearing of the people; and they said, "All that the LORD has spoken we will do, and we will be obedient."

Live By The Spirit

Galatians 5:25 NAS
If we live by the Spirit, let us also walk by the Spirit.

As I read the scripture of Galatians, my thoughts settled on chapter 5, verse 25. This is what came to my thinking: "If we live by the Spirit, let us also be guided by the Spirit."

Doesn't it stand to reason that if we are guided by the Spirit, we should be living and walking by the Spirit? I cannot see someone **truly living** by the Holy Spirit… and **not** being guided or walking by the Holy Spirit… unless… one is guided by self. Then they are walking by self and they stray from living by the Spirit.

The Bells

I heard the bells as I lay awake.
In tears I heard them ring.
They played a song I've never heard.
I wonder what it means.

As I lay within the silence of darkness, I long for comforting silence… for my silence yells at me to stop.

Stop? Stop the silence?

I asked "Why should I stop the silence?

The reply I heard within my heart was: "Silence can be comforting, but the yelling must stop because with so much noise you will not hear the comforting sounds from God! Hear the bells within your darkness and rest within your knowledge."

Proverbs 3:5 KJV
Trust in the LORD with all thine heart;
and lean not unto thine own understanding.

Recognize It

A friend and I were talking. He said: "You do not need to seek the way. The Way of life has already come to you. You only need to recognize it."

How true. Thank you Lord. Amen.

> *Mark 10:52 KJV*
> *And Jesus said unto him, Go thy way; thy faith hath made thee whole. And immediately he received his sight, and followed Jesus in the way.*

Victory

When substance abuse runs rampant through life, there are no winners.

Victory comes to all when abuse is placed beyond ones reach... within the care of Love Incarnate which is Jesus Christ. Placing the substance within the boxes of humanness only creates human temptation, but humanness is understood by Jesus. He too, was human.

Resisting the substance that causes our abuse is a daily walk... no matter what our abuse may be. "What substance," you ask?

Think not that you have none, for the truth resides within each human.

> *Psalm 143:10 NRSV*
> *Teach me to do your will, for you are my God. Let your good spirit lead me on a level path.*

Build An Ark

We all go through "drought periods" in our lives. I have found, when you experience a drought period you need to build an ark. Yes, build an ark! It is in the building that we may find the love and compassion lost during our hot drought conditions.

What I am saying is to find a worthwhile project and work on it... even if only "work on it" means that you work on it for a short period of time each day. If you are so dry that you are not able to get out of your home... bake something and after "baking something", share it! Share it with a neighbor, a friend, a family member or even someone on the street that might not think you are strange.

If you sew, do craft projects, paint, crochet or knit, start making something. Have faith that God will use your "ark" to help others. If you do none of these things and you cannot think of anything to "build," just look around yourself. What do you see? Does your church office need some help? Could your Animal Shelter use some support? The Hospital? Troubled youth? Women's Shelter? You need not feel you have to save the world just now... just yourself. What in your community would be fun to help with? Go ahead–build that ark! Noah started with a hammer and some nails. All we have to do is start our "ark" and have faith in God. God will do the rest.

The Beauty Within Each Season

I enjoy photography and through photography I have been able to see The Beauty Within Each Season. Becoming aware of what is set before me within the seasons; I realize that sometimes we take sunshine and flowers for granted. We forget to stop and enjoy what God has created within the folds of life... until life changes and drought or even torrential rains draw our attention to the balance of nature.

Nature is a constant reminder that life is in order.

One season comes and goes until the next season allows us a new perspective of what is set before us.

We need not go through each season and point to its beauty. For if you look closely... you will be able to see all there is to see.

Thinking of each season, it seems to me, that the most difficult season is a winter of cold, dreary times. Even then, you can gain comfort in seeing all there is to see when the bare branches reach unto the heavens... and have nothing to hide. There is a season for everything under the sun.

Remember to look for THE BEAUTY WITHIN EACH SEASON.

Ecclesiastes 3:1 RSV
FOR EVERYTHING there is a season,
and a time for every matter under heaven.

A New Tomorrow

So humbly I bowed
  in that stable so small.
So humbly I bowed.
  I gave Him my all.

Oh how I grieved
  that I did not have more.
Oh how I grieved.
  Tears rushed to the floor.

His eyes looked at mine.
  He knew all my sorrows.
His eyes looked at mine.
  A new tomorrow!

2 Corinthians 5:17 KJV
  Therefore if any man be in Christ, he is a new creature: old things are passed away; behold, all things are become new.

You Fill Me With Happy

As I read through a spiral notebook, I came upon some cute little sayings. I am not sure which friend I was thinking of at the time, but I got to thinking about friends in general and what they meant to me.

This is what I found in my notebook:

Having you as a friend… fills me up with happy.

When God created beauty, He was thinking of a friend like you.

I do not know about you, but I certainly would like to be a friend like I was thinking about at the time!

To be a friend is not always easy.

Friends should try to be there for each other in good times as well as the hard times. Friends will let friends cry if they need to cry. Laugh when they want to laugh and just hang out with them if necessary.

What kind of friend are you?

Do you fill your friends with happy as well as beauty?

Proverbs 15:13 NAS
A joyful heart makes a cheerful face, but
when the heart is sad, the spirit is broken.

What You Are

I saw a man; a woman and two children get out of a car. I also saw an older woman run from a house. They embraced each other with joy! I wondered who these people could be and what they represented.

As I watched the scene before me, a friend put his arm around my shoulder. He softly spoke these words to me:

"Love is only what you can give from the feelings within your heart. Love is what makes you what you are."

> *1 John 4:12 NAS*
> *No one has beheld God at any time; if we love one another, God abides in us, and His love is perfected in us.*

The Edge Of The Storm

We were returning home from visiting my husband's mother. The sky was ominous and the clouds seemed to come alive within dark skies. Severe weather warnings were broadcast over the radio. I watched the sky as we traveled along the edge of the storm.

We raced toward the comfort of our home. We hoped to get to the comfort of home before the storm overtook us... the race was on!

As I watched the edge of this storm, its beauty was breathtaking. The sky took on a golden glow as the sun reflected off the clouds. I found myself watching the sky as if I were in a trance. A thought broke my concentration on the sky.

Was the thought within my heart or was it within my mind? Maybe the thought came from the sky and clouds. It does not matter.

I heard these words within my being: "The edge of the storm has a beauty of its own. Before the grey clouds consume your world, embrace the beauty before you."

Have you ever noticed how golden the edge of a storm cloud can appear? Its beauty matches no other. As the storm clouds of life attempt to overtake you... look for the beauty that only God can create. Amen.

Matthew 8:27 RSV
And the men marveled, saying, "What sort of man is this, that even winds and sea obey him?"

Answered Prayers

O' Lord, my heart does cry
And joy will not show her face.
But with you, my Lord, deep inside
I will forever keep my faith.

It might be days, it might be hours.
The rain shall water waiting flowers.
Then the sun shall ease my pain.
And I will turn and laugh again.

Until then, my Lord, I ask and pray
You send a friend to comfort, to stay.
And knowing, You do answer prayers.
I sit and wait for those that care.

Psalm 138:3 NKJV
In the day when I cried out, You answered me, and made me bold with strength in my soul.

One Upon The Other

I was on a winding road.

As I walked over a hill, I saw a beautiful painting before me.

In the painting, the mountains were layered... one upon the other.

Their color was breathtaking.

I stood speechless. The one that walked with me smiled as I stood in silence. Then he said:

"There are layers of mountains that reach to the sky. Each one becomes a lighter color the closer you are to God. Reach for the heights and the darkness of your mountains will lighten."

Philippians 3:14 RSV
I press on toward the goal for the prize of the upward call of God in Christ Jesus.

Quenching Your Thirst

I saw people in a sandy place.

The people did not seem happy.

As I watched, I could see the people were not at the beach, but in a desert. I also saw that they had become thirsty. The people began to grumble about having no water.

As I watched, a man hit a rock and water began to come forth.

I read about this story in the Bible. I knew about Moses hitting the rock with his staff. Why would I be seeing the story of Moses before me?

As I turned to walk away, another scene appeared.

People seemed to be extremely happy in this scene. The people were walking with a man. As the crowd got closer to me I could see they were walking with Jesus.

Their joy was overwhelming.

I could not take my eyes from what I was seeing. Someone from the crowd came to me and smiled. He said: "A daily walk with Jesus is more refreshing than a drink of water in the desert."

We all have times of walking in the desert.

Remember to take a walk with Jesus each day and you will not be thirsty.

John 4:13-14 NAS
Jesus answered and said to her, "Everyone who drinks of this water shall thirst again;

but whoever drinks of the water that I shall
give him shall never thirst; but the water that
I shall give him shall become in him a well of
water springing up to eternal life."

***

Sometimes, after experiencing the worst, we are able to feel the best... For we have known both.

***

I saw a Shepherd and a King standing together looking at a baby lying in a manger. A star was brighter than all the stars in the universe and angels sang with joy! Our Savior was born on this Christmas Night! Rejoice for Jesus is borne. Let us stand together with the Shepherds and Kings of old!

Phoebe

Romans 16:1-2 RSV

I commend to you our sister Phoebe, a deaconess of the church at Cenchreae, that you may receive her in the Lord as befits the saints, and help her in whatever she may require from you, for she has been a helper of many and of myself as well.

This scripture says much to us all. It tells how Phoebe did her best to help others. She even had the opportunity to help Paul. Although the main part of the scripture is concerning Phoebe and her way of doing the Lords work, two small words caught my attention.

Those words were "help her."

How often do we look at the workers of our church and think that they are special people? Those special people seem to find time and energy to do so much. How many times have we wanted to be just like them? How many times have we thought that they did not need our help?

In this scripture Paul presented a person who did much for many people, but he also asked the people to "help her." I am sure we should interpret this in a way that says we need to help her minister to others. I know we should also do the things Phoebe did, but I feel there is another interpretation which is often not seen. To me this scripture also says that the people who are doing things for many also need those things done for them.

When was the last time you sent a card which says "Have a nice day" to someone that seems as if they did not need it? When was the last time you listened to a person who seemed as if they were so strong that they could handle anything? When were you there to help them in a crisis? When were you shocked that they asked for help? When did you say "I didn't think a person like you needed help?"

Paul said for us to "help her." He said this because he realized that she is just like you and me. He realized that she was not a superwoman who did not need support, comfort or a kind word from others. Yes, Paul knew she worked at what she did.

Just like you and just like me.

The Darkness

I wonder... Do you think the moon was bright in the sky that night or was the moon only a sliver of its brightness?

I suppose the light was just the right amount of light... Just enough light for a small band of men to find their way to a garden. The men knew where they were going, but only One knew why. Darkness settled in as the men slept... except for One.

"Can't you stay awake?" is asked within the darkness of the night, but the darkness will not allow Jesus' followers the privilege of His company. The darkness drowns out prayers and pain. The men sleep in the darkness. That is how the darkness works.

Without the darkness, light might not be noticed.

Behold, a torch breaks the darkness... the black night of sorrow has begun!

> *Mark 14:41-42 NKJV*
> *Then He came the third time and said to them, "Are you still sleeping and resting? It is enough! The hour has come; behold, the Son of Man is being betrayed into the hands of sinners. Rise, let us be going. See, My betrayer is at hand."*

Fear Not

Genesis 15:1 RSV
AFTER THESE things the word of the LORD came to Abram in a vision, "Fear not, Abram, I am your shield; your reward shall be very great."

Thank you Lord for today, for today is today and not yesterday.

I see a cabinet. It is beautiful, but simple. I place my experience of 1979 gently into the cabinet. I close the doors and lower the latch. The latch is not locked. I will be able to see my treasure when necessary. My experience is guarded by the angles for it is of God. I shall go forward into time knowing the Holy Spirit is forever with me... for I feel His warm strength around me. His voice shall comfort me and I shall remember to look to God for what I need and not run all over this world looking for a human being to do the things which only God can do. I shall remember His voice in the church. That experience is mine to keep and hold close forever. I will not fear because the LORD is my shield. Amen.

Autumn Leaves

I can see the autumn leaves falling from the trees that prepare for winter winds and cold days. The sun makes the leaves glow with colors of red, yellow, brown and gold.

As I watch, a leaf gently glides upon the currants of life and lands upon the surface of a small stream. The stream carries the leaf through unknown territory until it tumbles over a waterfall. With resilience, the leaf remains on the surface of the water and joins more leaves as they gather together in a river of uncertainty. The beauty of the leaves cannot describe the blending of color upon the colors of creation.

Then, debris beneath the water's surface catches the leaf and it is cast into a pool of stillness. Unable to move, the leaf begins to decay... until a hand reaches into the stillness of the water and places the beauty of the frail leaf into a book where it rests for eternity.

So it is with all life.

> *Hebrews 11:3 NKJV*
> *By faith we understand that the worlds were framed by the word of God, so that the things which are seen were not made of things which are visible.*

Forever There

The Lord my God is forever there.
The Lord my God forever cares.
He knows my hurt.
He knows my pain.
He enables me to go on again.

He'll open the doors heavy with sorrow.
His light will show me another tomorrow.
I know my hurt.
I know my pain.
And with my Lord, I'll go on again.

1 Peter 5:7 RSV
Cast all your anxieties on him, for he cares about you.

I Can't

So often we say "I can't."

I can't change my ways. I can't write a book. I can't go back to school. I can't forgive someone. I can't love my neighbor. I can't do so many things that I long to do!

Why can't we do those things?

In Acts 12:7 Peter was bound in chains inside a prison. An angel came to release him from those chains. Just as Peter was released, we too can be released from our chains.

There are angels waiting to help us remove our chains. They may be seen in the form of a friend encouraging us to do the things we long to do. An angel may be seen in the form of a pet that has helped someone remember how to love and be loved. An angel could be in the form of a counselor or a member of the family.

There are many ways an angel can come to us.

If we allow the angels in our lives to help us, our chains can fall away and freedom will be seen before us.

Our prisons may continue to stand, but as we walk away from them we are able to see them in a different way.

Lord Jesus, help us to see the people you send into our lives that are willing to help us become free from our binding chains. Amen.

Acts 12:7 KJV
And, behold, the angel of the Lord came upon him, and a light shined in the prison: and he smote Peter on the side, and raised him up, saying, arise up quickly. And his chains fell off from his hands.

***

The song of my heart sings with joy and dances with heavenly music. Can you hear the music? Come... dance with me because the music is eternal!

***

Simple living ain't too bad! Plain simple living really ain't too bad!!

***

The spirit of those who have gone before us is with us also.

Jesus Knows

I saw a cocoon gracefully dangling from a sheltered part of a plant.

As I watched the scene before me, I saw movement from within the cocoon. Time passed and then I saw a beautiful butterfly emerge from the place where it had been sleeping. As my thoughts smiled upon what I saw, a friend allowed the butterfly to land upon his palm. He then lifted his hand and the butterfly flew into the gentle breeze.

My friend turned to me and said: "You do the same."

Jesus knows our potential. Many times we seem to sleep in dark cocoons. We struggle in darkness until one day we are able to break free from what has been holding us within ourselves. Once we emerge from our darkness, Jesus is waiting for us. Jesus smiles as we emerge into the Light and fly with our full potential into the breeze of life.

Thank you Lord Jesus for being there for each of us as we struggle to emerge from the darkness of our lives. Amen.

Jeremiah 17:7 NAS
Blessed is the man who trusts in the LORD and whose trust is the LORD.

Unending Love

I saw an image before me.

The image I saw was wonderful. It was an image of a man in a white robe. A glowing white light surrounded him. I knew in my heart and mind Who he was. I smiled and knowledge seemed to instantly engulf my being. The knowledge seemed to say: "The gift of love is more than the eye can see; the ears can hear; the nose can smell; the mind can comprehend or the heart can feel. The gift of love goes beyond life and when our soul touches the beauty of love... then we have touched love that will not die or fade from time."

Thank you Lord for your unending love for us. Amen

Psalm 73:26 NKJV
My flesh and my heart fail; but God is the strength of my heart and my portion forever.

Irritations

As I scratched an already angry area on my arm, I found a thought gently scolding me. The thought within my thinking said "Do not pick at open wounds. They will never heal if you do."

That thought is good advice for many areas of irritation in our lives.

How often do we dredge up memories of long ago and begin to dwell on them until they become open wounds once more? How often do we allow small things to become large... because we will not let them alone? Jesus does not want us to be in pain.

Jesus wants us to heal and become strong.

Jesus wants us to forgive.

Matthew 4:23 KJV
And Jesus went about all Galilee, teaching in their synagogues, and preaching the gospel of the kingdom, and healing all manner of sickness and all manner of disease among the people.

Choose A Path

I do not have to change the world.

I do not have to change a city.

I do not have to change one person.

If I keep God before me, He will do with my life as He chooses and I will follow His path. If the path becomes narrow, I know He has gone before me and made it wide enough for me to pass through. If the path becomes dark, I know He has made it light enough for me to see. If it becomes rough, I know He has made smooth the path chosen for me.

If I keep God before me, His path I can walk.

If I run before Him, He can only watch me choose a path that may be chosen for someone else. I know that if the wrong path becomes dark, narrow and rough, He will hold my hand.

If I put God before me, my path will be His. He will show me His way. If I run before Him, I may lose my way.

Exodus 13:21 RSV
And the Lord went before them by day in a pillar of cloud to lead them along the way, and by night in a pillar of fire to give them light, that they might travel by day and by night.

Growing With God

Growing with God is happiness and

                                         pain.

Contradictions and

                  compliments. Giving and

                                  receiving.

Ups and downs. In and out. Right side up and upside-down,

Over and under, loving and

                             laughing.

Caring and sharing, first and last

Mark 10:44-45
"And whoever wishes to be first among you shall be slave of all. For even the Son of Man did not come to be served, but to serve, and to give His life a ransom for many."

Holding Hands

The angels of heaven stand tall. Their wings spread across the country, casting a shadow for those who seek comfort.

From the heat, a shadow will travel down Main Street and join the hands of those who loved each other, but are still divided. This shadow will continue... joining towns to cities and cities to its country. The country shall stand firm and then that shadow will dissipate.

For a little while the hands, which were joined, will see each other... until they go their separate ways. Seeing no more.

The heat will return to normal as will those who held hands.

Philippians 2:4 RSV
Let each of you look not only to his own interests, but also to the interests of others.

Something New

I saw things that I had not seen before through the Scripture I read.

I decided to reread my morning devotional book that was dated from the year before. It was truly from the past century.

Each day I read what I thought I read the year before.

Each day I saw something new.

Why had I not seen the beauty within that Scripture last year? Why did that day's message speak to me in such a deeper way today? I know God speaks in His time and today was His time to speak to me through this Scripture. Wait… and God will reveal all things through His Son Jesus Christ the Holy One. The Spirit within you shall lead. Embrace The Spirit and obey.

Mark 1:8 NKJV
"I indeed baptized you with water, but
He will baptize you with the Holy Spirit."

Just Love

Isaiah 7:11-12 KJV
> *Ask thee a sign of the LORD thy God; ask*
> *it either in the depth, or in the height above.*
> *But Ahaz said, I will not ask, neither will I*
> *tempt the LORD.*

We did not ask for a sign.

We did not tempt the LORD.

We did not know of the Christ Child and so, God smiled upon a darkened world and gave us a star.

God gave us a sign even when we did not ask for the sign. The sign came in the form of a star shining in the night! The star came to rest over the place where Jesus slept as a tiny baby in his mother's arms.

The star, given to us many years ago, continues to shine.

That star glows among the piles of things we try to cope with during the Christmas Season. The star glows throughout each of our days and our nights.

Follow the star.

It is a sign given to us this day... no strings or ribbons attached... just love.

The Kingdom Of God

Luke 13:18-21 NAS

Therefore He was saying, "What is the kingdom of God like, and to what shall I compare it? It is like a mustard seed, which a man took and threw into his own garden; and it grew and became a tree; and THE BIRDS OF THE AIR NESTED IN ITS BRANCHES."

And again He said, "To what shall I compare the kingdom of God? It is like leaven, which a woman took and hid in three pecks of meal, until it was all leavened."

We have heard the parable where Jesus says that there are many rooms in his Father's house and that He is going to his Father's house to prepare a special room for each of us. *("In my Fathers house are many rooms; if it were not so, would I have told you that I go to prepare a place for you?" John 14:2 RSV)* What a wonderful Scripture! This Scripture teaches us that each person is very special to Jesus!

One morning, as I read *Luke 13:18 - 21*, I realized that these Scriptures reaffirm the abundance and greatness of heaven. Luke wrote that Heaven is like a mustard seed that grows to be a tree. He also pointed out that Heaven is like leaven that makes flour grow much larger than it originally had been. Both of these illustrations show us that heaven is large enough to sustain all who go to heaven. . . Not that I ever doubted the ability of heaven to hold all of us, but isn't it great that heaven enlarges its being to accommodate the guests who arrive daily?

Thank you Lord for making room in your home for each of us. Today is truly a day of thanksgiving. Amen.

***

In the billowing clouds an angelic trumpeter announced the presence of God and all bowed low. Look to the sky. What do you see within the clouds as they travel to untold places?

***

The light of God illuminates our world… For our world belongs to God. Yes, God is my world and He is also your world. Look and see what all God has created! Glory be to God in the highest! Amen.

Know Your Presence

Luke 9:9 RSV

   Herod said, "John I beheaded; but who is this about whom I hear such things?" And he sought to see him.

We certainly do not want to be thought of as the scripture above describes Herod, but let us look at the part where the scripture says, "And he sought to see him."

So often we are like Herod... We seek to see Jesus.

We have heard about this man named Jesus and the wonderful things he has done, but we often feel we have not seen Him.

How wrong we are!

We have seen Jesus and did not see Him. We have heard Jesus and did not listen. We have walked with Jesus and did not take his hand. Forgive us Lord. Sometimes we seek You for the wrong reasons and we become like Herod. Help us to seek You for the right reasons and know your presence. Amen.

Everybody Else

People seemed to be trying to be like each other.

One person put on a pink sweater.

To my surprise everyone found the same sweater and put it on. Another person then took off the sweater and placed it on a chair. Everyone did the same. This seemed to go on in one way or another for a period of time. I felt this scene could go on forever! I saw a friend smile from within the scene before me. He walked toward me and said: "Why be like everybody else? There is enough of "everybody else" within life. Be yourself. Be the person seen within yourself and you will rejoice with joy."

Lord, forgive me when I try to be someone other than myself. Amen.

Luke 9:25 RSV
For what does it profit a man if he gains
the whole world and loses or forfeits himself?

Do Not Fear

So often we say a prayer and impatiently wait for an answer.

We watch for signs of knowledge that will show us that the prayer was heard. We say "Are you really there? Do you really care? Will you help me? Will you help the ones I hold so dear?" But so often we do not stop and take time to listen. The answer is often given and never heard. The answers to our prayers bounce off self-made shields.

It is necessary to establish a time to share with God. A time to be still and listen. A time for God to talk to you and for you to listen to Him.

I sometimes fear what God might say. What if I do not get my way? God knows what is best for me. He overcomes my fears.

Thank you Lord. Amen.

Within my heart I heard Him say:

"Do not fear. I am still here to protect you. Your fear creates many problems, but the fear of centuries have destroyed much!"

He is right. Forgive me. Amen.

Isaiah 41:13 RSV
For I, the Lord your God, hold your right hand; It is I who say to you, "Fear not, I will help you."

Hemmed With Prayer

As I walked through a department store, I noticed a throw pillow with a cute saying upon it. I stopped to read the saying which said: "If your day is hemmed with prayer, it is less likely to unravel."

I really like this saying because I really like to sew, but what about the people who do not sew? What do they do to fix a hem when it begins to unravel?

These days there are many things on the market to repair a hem. Choosing one of them could be a challenge as well as figuring out how to use them!

Do I hear an Amen on that one?

I find that masking tape works really well for temporary disasters, but what works when we run out of easy gimmicks? Well, I have found the best solution for all of us... sewing buffs and those with two left thumbs! Take the garment or I might say... your day... to a professional. In this case you would take whatever is unraveling in your life to Jesus in prayer. Jesus will hear your prayers... Then you can go into your day knowing a Professional is always on the job to help you have the greatest day possible.

1 Samuel 15:27 NRSV
As Samuel turned to go away, Saul caught hold of the hem of his robe, and it tore.

A Light

God provides a light where we see none.

Sometimes we get caught up in self-made darkness and are unable to find our way out of it, but God is with us. He will provide a light where there seems to be none. God also provides His footsteps for us to follow. We must be willing to take hold of the Light and walk in His footsteps to a sunrise that is more glorious than we have ever seen.

Walk out of your darkness into His light.

Walk out of your darkness into His life.

> *John 8:12 NKJV*
> *Then Jesus spoke to them again, "I am the Light of the world. He who follows Me shall not walk in darkness, but have the light of life."*

Mothers Day

2 Timothy 1:5 NRSV

I am reminded of your sincere faith, a faith that lived first in your grandmother Lois and your mother Eunice and now, I am sure, lives in you.

I have a friend that has a mother named Eunice. Eunice is a faithful, beautiful lady... even in her aging years.

My friend reflects the faith of her mother and, I'm sure, her grandmother.

Although I do not know anything about her grandmother, I do know **her** and by knowing **her**, I feel blessed by her friendship.

My friend has not had a perfect life... Nor have any of us.

She has health problems and she overcame times of challenge... Just as many of us have, but even with those challenges, she has continued to be a faithful servant of God.

My friend takes care of her mother faithfully and gently. She is devoted to her husband and their dog... Her faith is beautiful and her prayers are a reflection of her faith.

It is Mother's Day... Although she does not have children, I know the generations of her loved ones will read the scripture above and smile as they think of a grandmother named Eunice and then, they will think of my friend.

Grace and Peace.

Believers

My world is yours and your world is mine.
Together we meet in reality.
The unbelievers will travel on their way
And take their unbelief with them.
But the believers shall remain and teach each other.

Matthew 28:19-20 RSV
"Go therefore and make disciples of all nations, baptizing them in the name of the Father and of the Son and of the Holy Spirit, teaching them to observe all that I have commanded you, and lo, I am with you always, to the close of the age."

God's Peace

I saw a beautiful mountain with a lake placed within its majestic beauty.

The lake appeared to be extremely deep. As I watched the beauty before me, I saw the lake become a river. The river seemed to become rough. It ran along jagged rocks and suddenly a waterfall could be seen in the distance. Once the river flowed over the rocks that were creating the waterfall, the river rushed downstream and eventually became still. As I watched the scene before me, a friend came from within the deepest part of the water and said:

"When you are at peace with God, the water runs still and deep. When there is no peace, the water is found to be rushing, splashing and pounding against rocks placed in its way. Allow the waters to become quiet once more and they will run deep. Do not create a dam. Dams create an unnatural flow to what is needed. Allow the water to run its course and then allow the water to pool into the deep part of your heart. Allow God's peace too still the raging waters set before you."

Thank you Lord for times of peace and serenity. Amen.

Luke 8:22-25 RSV
One day he got into a boat with his disciples, and he said to them, "Let us go across to the other side of the lake." So they set out, and as they sailed he fell asleep. And a storm of wind came down on the lake, and they were

filling with water, and were in danger. And they went and woke him, saying, "Master, Master, we are perishing!" And he awoke and rebuked the wind and the raging waves; and they ceased, and there was a calm. He said to them, "Where is your faith?" And they were afraid, and they marveled, saying to one another, "Who then is this, that he commands even wind and water, and they obey him?"

***

Beware of pride for it is the destroyer of men.

***

I seek the quietness of the Lord so that I might get through the noisiness of my day.

***

Patience is achieved by practice. Like many other talents patience is developed. When you develop patience, it will enhance your other talents. Patience is a great reward.

Vines And Trees

I looked into a densely wooded area.

The wooded area seemed dark and damp.

I did not want to walk into the wooded area for my feet were bare.

I did not know what may lie beneath the things that covered my path for I could not see the path leading me into the darkness of the unknown.

A friend came from the wooded area. He smiled as he stood beside me. He asked, "What grows deep within the woods... where the vines and trees cover the things that lie beneath them? Look beneath what covers your heart." Then he took off his sandals and walked where I did not dare walk.

Forgive me Lord when I am not willing to walk where you walk. Amen.

> *Song of Solomon 2:13 NIV*
> *The fig tree forms its early fruit; the blossoming vines spread their fragrance. Arise, come, my darling, my beautiful one, come with me.*

A True Friend

I will seek my Lord Jesus today.

I will try and talk to Him as a friend... because He is a friend.

He sits with me as a friend sits through hard times and happy times. He speaks to me in many ways and He listens to every word I say. I can pour out my deepest fears and then confess my worst secrets and He will not judge me.

He laughs with me and when I am quiet, He sits quietly beside me and we enjoy the quietness.

He is a true friend.

The truest friend one can have.

Proverbs 18:24 NKJV
A man who has friends must himself be friendly, but there is a friend who sticks closer than a brother.

Rocks

As I sat quietly, I heard these words within my heart: "You are not allowing my words to float. You keep weighing them down."

So often we tend to weigh down the words of the Lord. We tie them around us as if they were rocks. Then we try to walk with those rocks weighing heavy on our minds. When in truth, His words are light for those who carry them. The Lord will help us carry our load, but so often we do not see Him and we struggle to carry it alone.

Mark 4:16 RSV
And these in like manner are the ones sown upon rocky ground, who, when they hear the word, immediately receive it with joy.

Clouds

A cloud is often thought of as something dismal and gloomy. This thought often comes during the winter months when they arrive on the scene, laden with snow or rain. People also refer to bothersome times in their lives as cloudy and dark.

Poor clouds… They seem to have gotten such a sad reputation!

At this time, I would like to mention how useful a cloud can be. A cloud is God's natural blanket for us. When the sky is crisp and clear, the temperature can take a nosedive toward that zero mark and quite often goes well below. On the other hand, clouds do provide a warm blanket for us and keeps the temperature at a reasonable place on our thermometer.

I would like to suggest that when you wake up in the morning or glance outside to a sky filled with clouds; remember to think of them in a positive and useful way. Your day will be much brighter and the sunshine may shine through the clouds in ways you did not think were possible.

What a beautiful day! God has provided such a beautiful blanket for me to snuggle under. With the clouds in the heavens above, I will be warmer than last night… and God does know how much I like to snuggle!

Psalm 147:8 RSV
He covers the heavens with clouds, he prepares rain for the earth, he makes grass grow upon the hills.

New Perspective

We do not have to wait for a New Year to begin to start a new outlook on life. Every minute is a new beginning for us. I know I am not saying anything new or unique, but we seem to lose sight of what life can be about.

Sometimes we get caught up in our daily lives to the extent that we do not see beyond what we do each day.

Sometimes it is good to see what we do from a new perspective.

How might we accomplish such a feat? Shall we meet new people and listen to what they have to say? I mean... really listen? Shall we listen with ears of contentment to what the Lord says to us through prayer, study and meditation? What will you see between the folds of time within the time of your day? What new sights are before you? Look out your window and see with newness and wonder.

What way will you see life?

It is good to have a new perspective. Amen.

Matthew 22:11 NRSV
"But when the king came in to see the guests, he noticed a man there who was not wearing a wedding robe."

Have Boldness

Hebrews 10:19-22 NAS

Since therefore, brethren, we have confidence to enter the holy place by the blood of Jesus, by a new and living way which He inaugurated for us through the veil, that is, His flesh, and since we have a great priest over the house of God, let us draw near with a sincere heart in full assurance of faith, having our hearts sprinkled clean from an evil conscience and our bodies washed with pure water.

As I read the scripture above, understanding was placed within my thoughts.

Now, so there is no misunderstanding, I would like to say that I do believe total understanding belongs to God and God gives understanding to different people at different times.

When you perceive a different understanding as you read the pages of the Bible... if your understanding is true... it is of God.

This is the understanding placed within my thoughts on the day I read the pages of the Bible before me: "Therefore, brethren, have boldness." For those who cower in darkness shall stay in darkness until they take the hand of the Christ that extends love unto their being."

Take my hand into your hand Lord Jesus and allow me to feel your love. Amen.

I Rode The Thunder

I rode the thunder as it rolled across the sky.
The clouds felt my pain and started to cry.
The clouds felt my sorrow and held me close.
They allowed me to ride as long as I chose.

Some things are healed as soon as they're told.
Some things aren't healed until you are old.
The time will come when you will let go.
And then the thunder you no longer will hold.

2 Samuel 22:12-14 RSV
He made darkness around him his
canopy, thick clouds, a gathering of water.
Out of the brightness before him coals of fire
flamed forth. The LORD thundered from
heaven, and the Most High uttered his voice.

A Helping Hand

I noticed people looking at the tall buildings surrounding them. Some people would stop and take pictures of what they saw. Other people would admire what stood before them and still others would sit on benches, walls and other comfortable items that were found within their path. Time seemed to slow as the people slowed. Occasionally, someone would rush past the people resting within the spaces of time.

I began to wonder what was taking place before me. Suddenly a thought entered my thinking. This is what I heard:

"We are travelers in the spaces of time where life is known to those who live it. To many people life is seen as a tourist sees rather than a life traveler. Travel into the lives of those traveling toward you and see what you can do. Many need a hand to help them within the spaces of time. Look and see… become as a traveler, not a tourist."

Isaiah 30:21 RSV
And your ears shall hear a word behind you, saying, "This is the way, walk in in it," when you turn to the right or when you turn to the left.

Many Points, One Cross

I was talking to a friend one day and realized that we did not see and feel the same points in our conversation. This did not bother me because I realized that there is more than one point on a cross. We are part of the same cross and there are many points on that cross. I will allow her to see and feel her points of the cross and I pray that she will allow the same for me. Her points will touch those areas of her life which are to be touched. Mine will do the same. Let your points join ours because we are all part of the same cross. Amen.

> *Acts 28:25 NKJV*
> *So when they did not agree among themselves, they departed after Paul had said one word: "The Holy Spirit spoke rightly through Isaiah the prophet to our fathers.*

Five Talents Or One Talent?

Matthew 25:14-18 RSV

"For it will be as when a man going on a journey called his servants and entrusted to them his property; to one he gave five talents, to another two, to another one, to each according to his ability. Then he went away. He who had received the five talents went at once and traded with them; and he made five talents more. So also, he who had the two talents made two talents more. But he who had received the one talent went and dug in the ground and hid his master's money."

I am sure we have all read the scripture above many times and each time we read it… it touches our hearts. This morning as I was reading, my heart saw what lay before me, in a little different way than when I read it in the past. As I read, I became aware that God gave each servant the talents that he could handle without over extending the amount of stress within that person.

Let us consider what might have happened if God had given five talents to the person that received the one talent. How would that person have reacted? He was not able to handle the one talent given to him. Four more talents would have been too great a burden on him.

On the other hand, the one with five talents would not have had enough to do if he had only been given one talent. Example: My friend's son was given more work to do in class when he was in the third grade. His teacher recognized that when he had finished his work before the others were finished, he became bored and disrupted those that were trying to finish their assignment. By giving her child more work to do in areas that he enjoyed, he stayed out of trouble. My friend was thankful to her son's teacher for being so perceptive.

By giving each person the talents suitable to their wellbeing, they will accomplish what God wants them to accomplish, but be aware that God wants us to use our talents... not bury them. If we bury them, we also bury their intended purpose.

***

When you show love in any way, shape or form, it will reflect the love within you to those you show love to.

***

A heater comes on at timed intervals to warm you. So it is with LOVE.

Perfection Not Required

I saw some people coming and going from a church.

It did not matter which way they were coming and going, but they would stop, look at a sign just outside the church door and smile. I walked over to the sign to find out what it said. As I stood before the neatly printed sign, a friend joined me. The sign simply said "Perfection not required." As I looked at my friend, he smiled.

> *Psalm 72:13-14 NKJV*
> *He will spare the poor and needy, and will save the souls of the needy. He will redeem their life from oppression and violence; and precious shall be their blood in His sight.*

Obedience

Many years ago I wrote this simple thought in my journal: "Each step of obedience leads to greater faith." How wonderful it is to come across something I had written years ago and have it speak to me today.

I had also sketched several art ideas below the thought written on yellowed pages. The art images were nothing new. They simply reflected thoughts of many other artists over the years. One sketch showed two sets of footprints going somewhere and then the two sets of footprints turned into one set of footprints... Only to return to two sets of footprints once more. I am sure you have seen that image of art many times.

The other image was of steps. Interestingly enough, I am working on a Bible study with the same image shown within the workbook. The one difference between my image of steps and the Bible study image is that my sketch showed Jesus as Alpha and Omega. I placed Jesus at the bottom of my steps and also at the top of the steps. In between were words like hope, faith, love, forgiveness, etc. As I continue to do what needs to be done in my workbook, I am sure their steps and the steps within my notebook will look the same.

In order to walk those steps we need to be mindful of where we have been and where we are going. Jesus is always the First and the Last and I will listen closely as I try to be obedient to His movement in my life. Amen.

Revelation 1:8 NKJV

"I am the Alpha and the Omega, the Beginning and the End," says the Lord, "who is and was and who is to come, the Almighty."

***

Lord, give me the wisdom to know what is right and the understanding to know what is good. Amen.

***

Bringing out the best in others will bring out the best in you. Am I willing to bring out the best in others?

***

Take care of one thing at a time and time will take care of each thing you do.

Your Gift

Christmas is joy. Christmas is love.
Christmas is a gift from Heaven above.

A gift to be opened by each of our hearts.
A gift of love that will not depart.

Your heart will fill with a love so great.
Your Savior has come to show you His way.

So open your gift from Heaven above.
Experience the Lord. Experience His love.

The experience is worth any pain that you hold.
The Lord has come. The story told.

Jeremiah 31:25 RSV
"For I will satisfy the weary soul, and every languishing soul I will replenish."

The Gift Of Grace

I came across an interesting thought in one of my notebooks.

As I read the words within the notebook they made me smile. I am not exactly sure why I wrote this thought: "What is Grace? I think grace is not thumping the cat for getting the ham off of the table!" (Do you think my cat had helped himself that day?)

I guess not thumping the cat is as good an explanation for grace as any that I can think of! If you are an animal person, you certainly can understand what is meant by the thought.

I wonder if God put those thoughts within my mind to show how simply Grace can be explained to others. I am sure God is sometimes tempted to thump us when we do something He does not approve of. Thank you Lord for the gift of Grace. Amen.

John 1:16 RSV
And from his fullness have we all received, grace upon grace.

Butterflies On The Wind

In this booklet you will read several devotionals connected to my experience with two Appalachian Service Project (ASP) trips with my church. One was an Adult ASP trip and the other was a Youth ASP trip.

When we returned from our ASP adventure, some of the youth gave a testimony about their experience during the Sunday morning church services. One of the youth told about a "God Moment" that she and her team had experienced. She said that progress on the home they were repairing was going slow and tedious. The team began to get discouraged with their progress. Then they noticed movement in the grass. It was a swarm of butterflies! Their team's name was "The Butterflies" and so, this "God Moment" renewed their spirits and they were able to continue with a new determination and finish the project they were given.

I am sure the butterflies did not remain in the grass. I can see them taking to the wind... bringing joy to all who see them.

Just as the butterflies took to the wind, so do those who work on the Appalachian Service Projects. Once their work is done, they go home and share their stories of joy and service.

Let us remember all those who volunteer on the Appalachian Service Projects as well as those who work on many other worthwhile projects throughout the world... Each person is a witness for Christ. Think of them as they become "Butterflies On The Wind" and spread hope to others.

Romans 12:4-8 RSV

For as in one body we have many members, and all the members do not have the same function, so we, though many, are one body in Christ, and individually members one of another. Having gifts that differ according to the grace given to us, let us use them: if prophecy, in proportion to our faith; if service, in our serving; he who teaches, in his teaching; he who exhorts, in his exhortation; he who contributes, in liberality; he who gives aid, with zeal; he who does acts of mercy, with cheerfulness.

***

Sometimes to forgive and forget is not possible, but to forgive and remember is within reality.

***

Remember to decorate your life with sunshine and flowers.

Something Different

You will find something different about this booklet of thoughts and poems. I am including the expressions of a few friends! I happily share these expressions because they are expressions from the heart. I thank each and every one of these friends for allowing me to include a small portion of their heart with you.

God prepares your heart to receive His grace and peace. Do you receive all that He gives to you? Do you hear His voice as you walk through His day? Do you feel His presence in the life set before you? Do you share His thoughts with others? Most of all do you share His thoughts with yourself or do you simply cast them aside... not knowing where those thoughts come from?

> *Deuteronomy 5:23-24 NKJV*
> *"So it was, when you heard the voice from the midst of the darkness, while the mountain was burning with fire, that you came near to me, all the heads of your tribes and your elders. And you said: "Surely the LORD our GOD has shown us His glory and His greatness, and we have heard His voice from the midst of the fire. We have seen this day that God speaks with man; yet he still lives."*

Love Is Enough

I wanted to bring happiness to those around me.

I asked a friend what I could do to bring happiness to those God had placed within my care. I said: "If I move mountains for them, will they be happy?" He said: "You can try." I tried to move a mountain. The mountain did not move.

"If I calm a raging river, will they be happy?" "You can try." I found a raging river and placed rocks within it. The river simply pushed the rocks to one side.

"If I give them all my fortune, will they be happy?" "What fortune will you give them?" "I will give them what I have. Will this make them happy?"

"Tell me, please: What can I do to make them happy?" "One does not need to do great things in order to bring happiness to others. Love is enough."

Proverbs 3:13 RSV
Happy is the man who finds wisdom, and the man who gets understanding.

The Red Horse

Zechariah 1:8 RSV

"I saw in the night, and behold, a man riding upon a red horse! He was standing among the myrtle trees in the glen; and behind him were red, sorrel, and white horses."

Revelation 6:4 RSV

And out came another horse, bright red; its rider was permitted to take peace from the earth, so that men should slay one another, and he was given a great sword.

Have you seen the red horse?

He is found standing among the myrtle trees in Zechariah 1:8.

In Revelation 6:4 the red horse is permitted to take peace from the Earth.

Yes, my friends, I feel you have seen the red horse and its rider!

Does the red horse ride this very day upon our land? Does the red horse bring fear as he rides through the countryside? I expect the red horse is not as gentle as we would hope, but still he rides. He rides from within the Old Testament unto the end of the New Testament.

How do you feel as you gaze upon the red horse? Will you run from the sight of the red horse?

Are you human?

I expect I might do what I am led to do at the time. I hope I turn and help others in the wake of the red horse's ride.

But if I am unable to help... I will find peace within the arms of my Lord Jesus.

Forgive me. Amen.

***

For centuries the mountains have inspired the world, challenged the world and continues to be strong in the world. Where do you see mountains in your life? How high have you climbed to overcome each one of those mountains? Remember to keep on climbing... for climbing strengthens you as you climb.

***

Some children can be a challenge, but remember so were we and as we are seen as children of God... many of us probably still are seen as a challenge.

Rescued

I have a friend that rescues dogs. Her passion is Schnauzers. Sometimes she may have about eight Schnauzers in her care. Many times she is able to find homes for the dogs, but until a caring family adopts them she takes them into her home as if they were her own.

One day she showed me a picture of a pile of fur. She said the pile of fur was found along the side of the road. No one knows why the dog became homeless, but thankfully the little dog was rescued. My friend continued with her story and said, "Guess what they found under all that fur!" She then handed me another picture. She smiled as she said, "A Schnauzer!" The dog now lives with her. He has a warm bed to sleep in, good food to eat and love shared by both.

Someone was able to see beyond the ball of matted, dirty fur. They saw potential in this small creature and took time and energy to see what might be underneath the obvious.

The actions of the ones caring for the dog reflect the care that Jesus gives to each of us. Jesus sees beyond our shaggy appearances. He sees the beauty in which we are created.

Thank you Lord for rescuing me from my dirty, shaggy condition. Thank you for all those that do Your work. Amen.

Colossians 1:13-14 NAS

For He delivered us from the domain of darkness, and transferred us to the kingdom of His beloved Son, in whom we have redemption, the forgiveness of sins.

***

Love is a jewel that sparkles within and glows on the outside.

***

The sun within someone's day can be the smile you send their way. Who needs a smile today? Look and see who may be within your reach?

***

A rainbow is merely an upside down smile. Go ahead… smile!

Empty Your Mind

I sat watching what was before me.

A man emptied his mind as he turned to greet those around him. The man embraced one person and then he embraced another. He continued embracing everyone that was brought into his life. Joy filled his heart and his mind was satisfied. How strange, I thought. What does it mean?

A friend sat beside me.

He quietly said: "Sometimes we need to empty our minds and fill our hearts... then love will overflow."

Lord, I will empty my mind often and I will fill my heart with the love You give to each of us. Let me grow in You Lord. Let me embrace the people You place within my life. Amen.

Romans 15:13 RSV
May the God of hope fill you with all joy
and peace in believing, so that by the power
of the Holy Spirit you may abound in hope.

Discover

In the old there is new.
There are many things
 to be discovered.
 When you think you know a book
 from cover to cover,
You will discover
 you do not know it at all.
Then...
 You will discover the new.

Mark 4:22-23 NKJV
"For there is nothing hidden which will not be revealed, nor has anything been kept secret but that it should come to light. If anyone has ears to hear, let him hear."

The Glory Of God

I saw a cloud that looked as if someone took a brush and gently brushed rays of light toward the barren ground. It seemed as if the beauty of the moment was saying that the glory of God reaches through the clouds to touch our hearts with joy and love.

I have seen this scene many times and in many places. It never ceases to amaze me as I look upon its glory.

Thank you Lord for the beauty you set before me. Amen.

Exodus 33:18 NAS
Then Moses said, "I pray Thee, show me Thy glory!"

No Greater Blessing

We were looking into a room with many riches. My friend quietly shared these words with me:

"Do not just count your blessings... Share them! Share of yourself. There is no greater blessing. You have more riches stored inside than all the treasure storehouses in the world. Look within and share your blessings. You have much to give. As your riches are used, they will be replaced... more will be added."

Thank you Lord. I will count my blessings and then share them with others. Amen.

Malachi 3:10 RSV
   Bring the full tithes into the storehouse, that there may be food in my house; and thereby put me to the test, says the LORD of hosts, if I will not open the windows of heaven for you and pour down for you an overflowing blessing.

Healed By Time

A friend was with me.

We sat looking into a beautiful canyon. We spoke quietly so we would not disturb the beauty set before us. He told me that he will heal my deepest wounds... like crevices within the earth, healed by time.

So it is with life.

Thank you Lord for allowing time to heal the deep crevices within my life. Amen.

Matthew 19:26 RSV
But Jesus looked at them and said to them, "With men this is impossible, but with God all things are possible."

Just Like Abraham

Hebrews 11:8 NKJV

By faith Abraham obeyed when he was called to go out to the place which he would receive as an inheritance. And he went out, not knowing where he was going.

Have you ever wondered where you are going? Sometimes we ask ourselves questions like: "Where will my job take me? Where will I see beauty within the feelings that I find within myself? When will I feel peace about the people I see throughout my life? Whom will I spend my life with? Will I have children? Does God really care about me? Will I wander forever... not knowing the questions of life?"

"There are so many questions about life! Sometimes I feel that I am going somewhere... but I do not know where I am going! Where am I going anyway? Where exactly am I going!?"

Many times we cannot see where we are going.

Many times we just have to trust in God who calls us to follow Him.

Just like Abraham we must step into life in faith. In faith we will receive the inheritance God longs to give to each of us.

Obey Gods calling when He calls you. Obey the words God has spoken within your heart.

God is calling you! Can you hear His voice?

Will you go?

Knowledge Of Life

Proverbs 3:5-6 NKJV
Trust in the LORD with all your heart,
and do not rely on your own insight. In all
your ways acknowledge him, and he will
make straight your paths.

As I read the scripture above I felt as if I heard these words within my heart:

"If you do not trust in the LORD, your own insight may blind you and your path will not be seen. Just as Jesus made the blind man see so shall He open your eyes to a path straight unto His knowledge of life."

LORD, I pray that You will show me Your way and help me trust You in all I do. Amen.

Bruises

I was in a gallery looking at works of art. This gallery was very interesting because the colors and shapes before me seemed to be alive. Those colors and shapes seemed to be changing right before my eyes. I saw colors of red, blue, purple, green and yellow. The colors blended and created designs within themselves.

The colors eventually faded away and a clean canvas hung on the wall before me.

All the colors and shapes eventually faded, but some of them took much longer than the others. As I pondered what I saw before me, the Caretaker came to my side. We watched some colors reappear on the canvases. As we watched the colors make their interesting shapes, He answered the question I was about to ask. With concern in his eyes he said: "It depends on how deep the bruise goes as to how long the bruise will take to heal."

Sometimes we do not even know how we got our bruises, but Jesus knows our burdens (bruises) and He watches over them as the healing process takes place... no matter how long that healing process may be.

> *Isaiah 42:3 - 4 NAS*
> *"A bruised reed He will not break, and a dimly burning wick He will not extinguish, He will faithfully bring forth justice. He will not be disheartened or crushed, until He has established justice in the earth, and the coastlands will wait expectantly for His law."*

Under The Rug

I found myself frantically sweeping something under a rug. I was not sure what I was sweeping under the rug, but I knew that I did not want it within my sight.

Deep within my heart I knew that I should not be sweeping anything under a rug. I knew that I should be taking care of whatever I had swept under the rug in a proper manner, but I just kept sweeping. And sweeping. And sweeping!

Suddenly I was unable to walk on the rug. The rug had so much under it that I had to walk around it to get to where I was going. When I looked back at the rug, Jesus was lifting the rug with his strong hands. He picked up the rug and all the stuff I had swept under it. He shook the rug and everything disappeared before my eyes. He turned to me and said: "The things we sweep under the rug can build up until they tend to get in our way." Jesus placed the rug back into its place and walked into the beauty that surrounded Him.

Thank you Lord Jesus for taking care of what I sweep under rugs. Amen.

> *Isaiah 40:4 NIV*
> *Every valley shall be raised up, every mountain and hill made low; the rough ground shall become level, the rugged places a plain.*

Look Around You

As I walked into my thoughts, I began to see a road before me.

The road was straight and narrow.

I continued to walk through time and the road began to bend. The road became wide enough for me to see into the distance without peering through eyes shielded by the straightness of time from where I had just come. I looked at the land before me. I saw many things and I pondered their meaning.

As I wondered about what I saw, a friend approached me from the spaces between my thoughts and words. He began to walk with me. As we walked, He spoke words of love. He explained all that I saw. He told me how love can be found in the straightest places as well as in the areas that bend and curve into life. He said: "Love can be found in the dryness of life. Love can be found in the down pours of disaster. Love can be found within the lives of those around you. Look into all areas of your life. Find Me in all those areas and you will find Love."

Luke 10:33-34 RSV

But a Samaritan, as he journeyed, came to where he was; and when he saw him, he had compassion, and went to him and bound up his wounds, pouring on oil and wine; then he set him on his own beast and brought him to an inn, and took care of him.

Frosty

About a year ago a small dog named Frosty came to visit my home.

A friend was going to visit her family in New Jersey for Christmas and she needed a place for Frosty to stay while she and her family were gone. I volunteered to dog-sit for Frosty until his family returned home the following week.

One morning a furry white dog bounced into my home and I will never forget all the fun we had! He is a mild-mannered dog and can do a number of tricks. He shook hands with my grandchildren, closed cabinet doors that were left open and played happily with those who were willing to play with him. We all became very fond of Frosty.

Frosty was a lot of company for me during that week following Christmas and I never expected to become so sad when time came for him to return to his family!

As I said a friendly good-bye to Frosty, he seemed to understand what I was saying when I told him that his family was on their way to pick him up. He turned his head one way and then the other. He listened to what I had to say, gave me a gentle kiss and turned to look out the window. Frosty remained at the window until he saw a familiar car turn into our drive. He recognized the ones that he loved and his joy was a wonderful sight!

I knew that I would miss Frosty, but I also knew his family had missed him even more than I could ever miss him. There is nothing more special than family... no matter where they are!

I will always remember a special Christmas with a little white dog named Frosty and I am thankful that God provided an opportunity for me to dog-sit.

Just as Frosty became part of my life and my heart, so it is with all those entrusted into my care by my Heavenly Father. Remember your family members, friends, pets; acquaintances... all are here for a short time. Enjoy their time within your life for they will go home one day.

> *2 Corinthians 5:6-8 RSV*
> *So we are always of good courage; we know that while we are at home in the body we are away from the Lord, for we walk by faith, not by sight. We are of good courage, and we would rather be away from the body and at home with the Lord.*

Many Faces

A church sees many faces in its days.
It sees those faces in many ways.
The faces seem to come and go.
Those faces the church will long to know.

It sees them smile and often say:
"I hope you have a very nice day."
It sees the faces sad and hurt.
Searching to know life's inner works.

It sees the young and sees the old.
It sees the feelings never told.
It sees the eyes that peek within.
It hears a whisper and sees a grin.

Yes, the faces seem to come and go.
Those faces the church will long to know.
But only God can reach within.
And start new life where sorrows have been.

Ephesians 3:20-21 NAS
Now to Him who is able to do exceeding abundantly beyond all that we ask or think, according to the power that works within us, to Him be the glory in the church and in Christ Jesus to all generations forever and ever. Amen.

You Built It

Psalm 127:1-5 NRSV
Unless the LORD builds the house,
*   those who build it labor in vain.*
Unless the LORD guards the city,
*   the guard keeps watch in vain,*
It is in vain that you rise up early
*   and go late to rest,*
eating the bread of anxious toil;
*   for he gives sleep to his beloved.*

Sons are indeed a heritage from the LORD,
*   the fruit of the womb a reward.*
Like arrows in the hand of a warrior
*   are the sons of one's youth.*
Happy is the man who has
*   his quiver full of them.*
He shall not be put to shame
*   when he speaks with his enemies in theate.*

You have built the gate I walk in and out of LORD. You created the garden I bow in. You give me strength to take the arrow of life and stand against the evil one. You light the fire that leads me through darkness and the darkness does not overcome me because I belong to You LORD JESUS. My sons are a blessing as I speak to my enemies in the gate. The gate is strong for You alone built it. Amen.

Peace

Luke 8:22-24 RSV

One day he got into a boat with his disciples, and he said to them, "Let us go across to the other side of the lake." So they set out, and as they sailed he fell asleep. And a storm of wind came down on the lake, and they were filling with water, and were in danger. And they went and woke him, saying, "Master, Master, we are perishing!" And he awoke and rebuked the wind and the raging waves; and they ceased, and there was a calm.

As I read the scripture above, I heard these words within my heart:

"The storm stilled and stepped aside."

"Peace appeared on the horizon and the calm came forth as a swan gliding across a small pond. The boat, no longer in danger, continued its journey. The once threatening water gently lapped at its side. The Lord rose and commanded peace to replace the chaos which surrounded him. The sky ceased rumbling and the dark clouds were gone."

Allow Jesus into the storms of your life.

Peace **will** appear on the horizon and the calm, which only Jesus can bring, will replace the chaos which surrounds you. Amen.

Questions And Answers

I was enjoying the cool fresh air after a storm had passed.

The leaves seemed to have more color once they had been washed clean. Clouds continued to move toward the East as if they were trying to catch the storm rushing into the distance. Raindrops dripped off flower petals and then splashed upon thirsty ground. Everything seemed perfect, but where was the rainbow? I had expected to see a rainbow in the sky above me!

As I looked for the rainbow, a friend joined me. He looked into the sky and said: "Rainbows are not always seen after a storm, but that does not mean that they do not exist. How would you prove the existence of a rainbow to those that have never seen one?"

What a hard question! He's asking me?

I guess the persons unable to see a rainbow would just have to trust me when I describe the rainbow to them. I suppose they would have to believe me by faith... not sight.

Lord, help me to believe by faith and not only by sight. Amen.

Job 42:4 NKJV
Listen, please, and let me speak; You said,
'I will question you, and you shall answer Me.'

Learning About Myself

I learn more and more about myself every day!
Some things I learn are good and some things I learn are not
as good as I would like.

I had an opportunity to join my church on an
Appalachian Service Project (ASP). I had heard so many
wonderful things about helping those in need that I just
knew I would have some wonderful tales to tell when I
returned home! That was not the case. I did not relate to
one of the people we were helping. I did not understand
my feelings and I became sad. When I returned home my
feelings darkened. I became so disappointed in myself that
I went to bed. I stayed in bed for most of the week.

Why did I react this way!? Why wasn't I on a "high" like
many people returning from a time of serving others? What
in the world was wrong with me? I did not have answers to
these questions and so, I slept some more. I finally got tired
of sleeping and turned to the One I felt as if I had let down.
"Lord, where did I fail You?" I prayed. His response was eye
opening to me. He showed me that I had allowed my past to
rule my present. In my past I relied only on myself. In the
past I felt that people should do things for themselves. I felt
that if you wanted a drink of water and there is no reason
why you cannot get it for yourself, then get it yourself... don't
expect me to get it for you! I'm not your servant!! That is
how I felt in my past. That is what seeped into my present.
That is what I needed to give up in order to be effective on
my next A. S. P. trip.

I saw that I was not to judge those placed before me. Jesus is the only one that will judge all of us.

Remember how I talked about my feelings of being your servant? Those feelings are found in my past. Those feelings are also found in my present because I have been reminded that I am a servant. A servant in Christ Jesus.

I have been called to serve each of you.

I am a servant of God.

I went to A. S. P. listening to the grandiose stories of others.

This time I will go to the Youth A S P seeing through the eyes of Christ and if I should hear a good story within my adventure... I will hear what Jesus would have me hear.

I will see what Jesus would have me see.

I will know what Jesus would have me know.

Lord, let me be the servant that You have called me to be. Amen.

Mark 9:35 RSV
And he sat down and called the twelve; and he said to them, "If anyone would be first, he must be last of all and servant of all."

Another Trip

Many times we find ourselves within feelings we are not comfortable with.

I found myself in an uncomfortable feeling about serving on an Appalachian Service Project (ASP) trip because of past experiences, but with God's help I was able to move on.

God gave me the strength to try again. I am thankful for the opportunity to serve Him... Not myself.

Within the pages that follow are thoughts and feelings about my Youth Appalachian Service Project adventure. I am thankful that God allowed me to experience life within the folds of other people that serve Him.

I am thankful to God for allowing me to have a New Day... a New Beginning! A fresh start. Amen.

> *Lamentations 3:22-24 NRSV*
> *The steadfast love of the LORD never ceases, his mercies never come to an end; they are new every morning; great is your faithfulness. "The LORD is my portion," says my soul, "therefore I will hope in him."*

Angels

I have, at times, heard people refer to other people as Angels.

When people are considered angels, they are usually doing or saying something good or worthwhile to or for someone else. Many times angels are people that volunteer for organizations. This could be said about the people working on the Appalachian Service Project (ASP).

Those who serve on an ASP team go into the Appalachian Mountains and repair homes. The teams serve for a week at a time. During that week friendships are usually made by those on the team and those friendships are a bonding that can last a lifetime. The bonding often occurs between individual team members, the people they serve and the teams from around the country.

As each team departs for home from their given home sites, smiles and sometimes tears are shared by all. The smiles we see are more than adequate for a week of our time to serve the Lord.

There are people all over the world needing our help. Let us reach out and help those within our reach.

How far can you reach?

If people serve the Lord in any way, they are truly angels doing God's work.

Thank you Lord for allowing me to serve as one of Your angels. Amen.

Philippians 2:3-4 NAS
Do nothing from selfishness or empty conceit, but with humility of mind let each

of you regard one another as more important than himself; do not merely look out for your own personal interests, but also for the interests of others.

***

Love is someone special. God loves you. You are special!

***

There is always room for another person in a heart that is at peace with God.

***

Plan for tomorrow, but concentrate on today for today is now.

Small Experiences

Small experiences make me smile just as much as large experiences can make me smile! Let me share one of my small experiences which were very large to me:

Four vans from our church caravanned toward our destination for ASP. I had never been in that part of the country and enjoyed watching the beauty set before me. Just as I was wondering how much farther we would be traveling, we turned off of an interstate highway and began winding our way toward our destination on winding mountain roads. As our four vans rounded a curve, we found ourselves behind four more vans.

What a sight it was for me!

Oh, what joy I felt deep within as I watched the eight vans weaving their way through the mountains to be the hands and feet of Christ! The memory of those eight vans is a beautiful memory! I will never forget the experience!

Thank you Lord Jesus for allowing me to have beautiful experiences... both large and small. Amen.

Isaiah 6:8 NAS
Then I heard the voice of the Lord, saying,
"Whom shall I send, and who will go for Us?"

Become A Missionary

To become a missionary in a country or area that has many resources is just as hard as becoming a missionary in an area that has very little resources.

When we seem to have an abundance of "things," it is hard to look at a neighbor across the street and wonder what it would be like to live in a home without holes in the floors, a roof that leaks, plumbing that does not work, no heat, no food or even to own a lawn mower.

It is hard to understand that our neighbors might be living in poverty.

ASP tries to help those that need to have their homes repaired. ASP is truly a missionary group. Oh, the team does not preach or teach the Gospel by speaking about Jesus... instead; they show the love of Jesus by their actions.

ASP teams accept others where they are at the moment and then make life a little more bearable.

There is much work to be done. There are many places to serve.

The missionary field is spread before you. Pick up a shovel or a hammer and walk with others through the field that only a true missionary can walk.

Thank you Lord for missionaries all over the world. Amen.

1 Timothy 6:18 NAS
Instruct them to do good, to be rich in good works, to be generous and ready to share.

96

From The Heart

Serving on an ASP team needs to come from the heart. ♥ Yes, service on an ASP team has to be given from the heart because your mind often sees the job placed before you as almost impossible. On the other hand, your heart knows how important it is to do the job, trusting that God will show you the way to accomplish the impossible.

When you are out on a work site, your mind tries to figure out challenging ways to make repairs to someone's home. Your mind just seems to work and work... until the job is done. It tries to figure out equations, it measures; it makes things fit properly, etcetera, etcetera, and etcetera!

Your mind has to work out many details about what needs to be done day by day. But what about your heart... what is it doing while your mind is working so hard? Are you serving with your heart as well as your mind? To really be on an Appalachian Service Project you have to begin with your heart and your mind will follow.

Your mind may tell you one thing as you look at impossible challenges within life, but God speaks to your heart and says: "You can do it" and then He shows your mind what to do. Listen for the word of the Lord and follow! Thanks be to God for all His mercies. Amen.

1 Chronicles 16:34 NKJV
Oh, give thanks to the LORD, for He is good! For His mercy endures forever.

Ice Cream

Can God be found in a cup of ice cream? Yes!

There was a small restaurant that served ice cream within walking distance of the school where our ASP teams slept at night. Some of the older participants (like me) rode to the restaurant in vans, but many of the youth walked. We seemed to descend upon the small eating establishment in waves which was good because I am not sure we would have all been able to fit in the restaurant at one time.

The owner of the restaurant seemed overjoyed with all the young people that volunteered their time in his community. He talked with many of them and you could see the joy he held within because of the smile on his face. The smile was wonderful!

Yes, the owner took delight in serving wave after wave of ASP workers as they came into his restaurant and on the last night of our week... he gave from his heart. He served each person ice cream and did not charge them.

The ice cream was free that night!

When we thanked him for his generosity, he said it was the least he could do for us. I am sure giving away free ice cream was not easy on his wallet, but when you give from the heart money does not always seem to matter because love matters more than money.

As I watched the restaurant owner serve the youth packed into his small place, I saw Jesus in his eyes. Yes, Jesus can be found in a cup of ice cream... or at least in the eyes of the one serving it.

***

Walking in the footsteps of God is not easy, but possible. Look for them!

***

We offer our gifts to God because He first offered them to us.

***

Running like a chicken is not always divine. A chicken doesn't know where he's running most of the time.

The Rain And The Sun

The rain came down. A tropical storm had sent rain over the Tennessee mountain range and we had not finished cutting wood for the home we were helping to repair. We heard that the rain would be "socked in" for two days so we made a makeshift tent to work under... And we prayed.

I'm sure all the teams were praying.

We wanted to accomplish our tasks and the rain held us back. As we prayed, we knew the rain was really needed in the area and we thanked God for all He provided. About noon the sky began to clear. Clouds parted and blue sky could be seen as the sun smiled upon us. We continued with our wood cutting and were able to stay on schedule.

Thunder rumbled in the distance as we thanked the Lord for providing the sun... and the rain. Amen. God's mercies never end.

Deuteronomy 28:12 RSV
The LORD will open to you his good treasury the heavens, to give the rain of your land in its season and to bless all the work of your hands, and you shall lend to many nations, but you shall not borrow.

They Are You

I normally do not mention names in the writing that is placed within my heart.

Although I normally do not mention names, today I feel that I would like to mention the names of the team members that I served with on an Appalachian Service Project during the Summer of 2005... and then I think again. Should I mention names or should I not mention names!?

As I ponder this urge to mention their names, I also remember all the other teams working for Christ and names become less important to me because all those that work for Christ are seen as equal in His eyes.

I will refrain from mentioning names.

Surely you already know their names because they are you!

1 Thessalonians 1:2-3 RSV
We give thanks to God always for you all, constantly mentioning you in our prayers, remembering before our God and Father your work of faith and labor of love and steadfastness of hope in our Lord Jesus Christ.

Our Own Personal Song

The music was wonderful. We listened with open hearts and some danced as we were entertained by a bluegrass band entertaining us on Culture Night.

The musicians and singers were wonderful!

This band was willing to give a little back to us as we tried to serve the Lord. In effect, they were serving the Lord in their own special way... Just like we were serving the Lord in our own special way.

We all have ways to serve our Lord Jesus. Let each of us step out in faith and sing our own personal song. Who knows, someone may even dance as they feel the joy we send forth.

Thank you Lord for allowing us to see you in others. Amen.

Psalm 100:1-2 NAS
Shout joyfully to the LORD, all the earth.
Serve the LORD with gladness; Come before
Him with joyful singing.

A Changed Heart

Each evening we had a time to express our feelings and tell about a time we saw Christ within our experience that day. One of the youth shared that, at first, she really did not want to be on this ASP trip. She even envisioned getting an injury that might leave a scar so that she could tell those at home of her adventure.

She continued witnessing.

As she talked, you could feel the change in her previous attitude. She said that she did not need a scar anymore. She said that she had received much more than a scar to prove how hard she worked during the week. We could see that her heart was overflowing with gratitude and love. As tears welled up within her eyes... I could see the love of Christ enfold her in His arms.

Jesus changed this young lady's heart and in doing so, He changed each person listening to her story. I pray she will continue to tell her story when she returns home. I pray that each of us will do the same. Amen.

1 Samuel 10:9 NIV
As Saul turned to leave Samuel, God changed Saul's heart, and all these signs were fulfilled that day.

Go Into Your World

The Appalachian Service Project (ASP) is not the only service project I have served with during the past several years. In Corpus Christi, Texas I served with the youth of Sea City Work Camp. Sea City Work Camp did the same things as those on the ASP teams, except they did the repairs to homes in Corpus Christi. Youth came from other states and they donated a week of their Summer vacation to help people in need... ASP does the same.

I can think of another group of volunteers that help people dwell in safety. That group is Habitat for Humanity.

Can you think of an organization that could use your help? I am sure you can add many more groups to my short list... so go into your world and help people live in safety through your service to those in need!

Psalm 4:8 NRSV
I will both lie down and sleep in peace;
for you alone, O LORD, make me lie down
in safety.

Time To Move On

It is time to move on from my Appalachian Service Project trips.

I hope you enjoyed the writing that was shared within this booklet and I look forward to sharing more thoughts within the pages of my next booklet. In God's love... Grace and peace to each of you. Amen.

2 Corinthians 4:15 RSV
For it is all for your sake, so that as grace extends to more and more people it may increase thanksgiving, to the glory of God.

Tall Meets High

Isaiah 55:9 NRSV
For as the heavens are higher than the earth, so are my ways higher than your ways and my thoughts than your thoughts.

How tall can you see?

I did not say how high can you see, I said how tall can you see? For seeing high is not high enough and seeing tall is only what you see placed before you until tall and high meet each other within life.

Lord, I pray that I am able to see what is placed before me and tall will meet high as I go through life. Amen.

Night And Light

When traveling through the night time hours, you see different things than when traveling in the daylight hours.

I took a trip to a town that was about three hours from where I lived. In order to be on time for a meeting which was to begin at eight o'clock in the morning, I left my home at five.

During the night time hours, I was able to see stars in the sky, a sliver of a moon that tilted to one side, illuminated signs with assorted messages, and places for me to stop for some coffee! I also noticed homes nestling in rural areas with their lights shining brightly as people began to prepare for the day. I saw many things during those darkened hours, but only if they were illuminated.

As the sun rose over the horizon, the beauty of its color made me smile. The day was beginning with a beauty of its own. When I stopped at a roadside rest area, I enjoyed seeing beautiful wild flowers that I was not aware of as I traveled in the darkness and I found myself smiling at people as they stepped from their cars. I would never smile at a stranger when stopping at a roadside rest area during the night… You never know who might be lurking in places that cannot be seen clearly!

Many things cannot be seen in the darkness!

The things we see in the night seem to shine brighter than the things we see in the light because the darkness makes us aware of the things we cannot see. The darkness illuminates the things chosen for us to see.

The sunrise brings light.

With the sunrise, we see much farther than in the darkness we have just traveled through.

Yes, we certainly see differently in the darkness than in the light, but there is beauty in both if we allow ourselves to see with the eyes of the Lord. Amen.

> *Genesis 1:3-5 RSV*
> *And God said, "Let there be light"; and there was light. And God saw that the light was good; and God separated the light from the darkness. God called the light Day, and the darkness he called Night. And there was evening and there was morning, one day.*

Seeds Of Creation

I saw a beautiful gift. As I watched, a flower grew from within the gift. Soon the flower began to wither and the seed within its beauty could be seen within its creation.

As I wondered about what I saw before me, a friend handed me the gift and said:

"Behold... the beauty of a flower. The flower is free for a short time and then it returns unto the earth which holds the seeds of creation."

Thank you Lord for Your Seeds of Creation. Amen.

1 Corinthians 2:12 RSV
Now we have received not the spirit of the world, but the Spirit which is from God, that we might understand the gifts bestowed on us by God

A Moment, A Life

I saw You for a moment.
I saw You in his eyes.
I never questioned who.
I never questioned why.

I saw You for a moment.
I knew that I was scared.
I knew You came to love me.
I knew You came to care.

I saw You for a moment.
You came to share my life.
That moment was forever.
That moment was my life.

A moment from God can be an eternity to life... for God holds eternity within His hands and embraces your life with eternity before Him.

Jeremiah 29:13 RSV
You will seek me and find me; when you seek me with all your heart.

Day By Day

Acts 2:46-47 RSV

And day by day, attending the temple together and breaking bread in their homes, they partook of food with glad and generous hearts, praising God and having favor with all the people. And the Lord added to their number day by day those who were being saved.

For me this scripture is an exciting one! I so very often get caught up in trying to want to save people on my own. I get so excited about how I feel and I so desperately want others to feel the same way. I want people to know that Christ is alive and will forgive the deepest sin they feel that they have committed. I want them to know that Christ is here now to save them. To hold them. To love them.

I get such an overwhelming feeling to want everyone in the world to know Christ in the same way I have been able to know Him. I often forget one important thing. I cannot save one person myself. Christ is the one who does the saving. He chooses the one to be saved. I can only be His tool if He chooses to use me. I can only be willing to do and say what Christ wants me to do and say. He will do the rest.

Stop and think about the scripture above... What a large burden is lifted from us. We do not have to do the saving of others. Trust a great and loving God to do what seems to be an impossible task!

I sometimes forget this and then I create a burden for myself when I should be finding peace and satisfaction. Only when I realize that it is not up to me to save anyone, am I able to let Christ do what He wants to do. He does the choosing. He does the saving.

One more beautiful thought in this scripture is that it reassures me that people are being saved by numbers day by day. How super! How great! The numbers are increasing every day and I do not have to do it all. In fact, none of us should feel as if we should do it all. We cannot do it at all. Only Christ can do it and He is... by numbers... day by day.

How exciting! How beautiful! I know God loves me today. I know this because He loves you too!

Can you tell how passionate I am about this subject? I hope so!

The Eyes Of God

I usually do not put dates on my writing.

The writing within my spiral notebooks seems to be timeless and timeless is where I leave them. Having said that the writing seems timeless, I sometimes lose a specific writing within the pages of undated writing.

No problem... unless I want to use a specific thought at a specific time!

The following thought is a good example of losing a specific thought for a specific booklet because it was supposed to explain a booklet named "Bullfrogs Are Beautiful Too," but I could not find it at that time. Let me share it with you now.

In my generation Jeremiah was considered a bullfrog because of a popular song called "Jeremiah Was A Bullfrog." Do you think the writer of this song realized how often gloom was portrayed within the writings of the book of Jeremiah in the Bible. Although there was gloom proclaimed in the book of Jeremiah, there was also hope portrayed within the same book. Jeremiah 29:11 says "For surely I know the plans I have for you, says the LORD, plans for your welfare and not for harm, to give you a future with hope." (NRSV)

Jeremiah had a lot to croak about... and he did just that. His words were spoken loud enough for centuries to hear his voice!

As we go into a new century, let us take our Lord and Savior Jesus Christ with us. We will surely need Jesus' love during the times that we feel like a bullfrog. Yes, proclaim the beauty seen within the pond before you. Look around and you will see butterflies, flowers, fish, dragonflies and many more that delight us all. What do you see around you today? Look closely. Look quickly. Most of all look with the eyes of God!

We have gone into the next century since this writing was written and the words still seem to ring true. We have seen many bullfrog days. We have heard many sounds of gloom. Has your pond survived the trauma of bombings, tornadoes, tsunamis, hurricanes, shootings, fire, death and heartache? Listen. What do you hear? Do you hear the bullfrog? The bullfrogs croak loudly and then they are gone. It takes courage to see beyond the noise of the day!

Another century is a long way into the future.

We must hear the words written years ago. We must also see the words and know they are as truthful today as they were then. Jeremiah brings us hope. Look within the pages of the Bible and see what you can see with your own eyes, but...

Most of all look with the eyes of God!

Jeremiah 29:12-13 NAS
Then you will call upon Me and come and pray to Me, and I will listen to you. And you will seek Me and find Me, when you search for Me with all your heart.

Rest

Have you ever thought about why you rest?

I never have thought about why I rest either, but as I sat quietly, a thought entered my thinking: "Rest. Rest my child, but do not give up the reason you rest."

Well, now I **am** wondering: Why am I resting? Am I tired? Am I escaping from many things running through my mind? Am I resting in the peace of God? Why am I resting? I really have not thought about why I am resting, but one thing I do know is that if I rest in the peace of God… I am resting right where I should be resting because all the other resting will be peaceful.

Why are you resting?

Thank you Lord for a time to rest. May we always rest in Your arms. Amen.

Colossians 3:15 NKJV
And let the peace of God rule in your hearts, to which also you were called in one body; and be thankful.

No Resentment

There have been many accounts of people seeing a vision of the Virgin Mary, mother of Jesus and I hear that those who have seen Mary's vision are never the same.

There are hundreds of people who travel great distances just to be near where the vision of Mary was seen… They long to be near Mary.

I know in my heart that Mary continues to bring hope, peace, healing and love to the world that her Son loves dearly. She is truly the mother of us all.

As I wrote the words above I heard these words within my heart:

"Mary was raised on high before giving birth to the Son of the Most High. She was smiled upon during motherhood and yet, Mary was pushed aside when her Son was placed upon the cross. She does not hold resentment toward those who did such a grievous deed… for she knows their hearts. Her mercies are greater than theirs and she will heal the hearts of those who cry." Amen.

Luke 1:28 KJV
And the angel came in unto her, and said,
Hail, thou that art highly favoured, the Lord
is with thee: blessed art thou among women.

Which Way Lord? Which Way?

Most of us have heard the saying "Where there is a will there is a way." This can also be said: "Where there is a will there is God's way.

I have mentioned that I do not date most of the things I write in my notebooks because I believe God's timing is timeless and He will direct me to write what is to be written in His time. Having said that, I will also mention I wrote the sentences above many years ago. Although those sentences were written years ago, they are also timeless in this time as well. Let me share what I wrote in my notebook for today:

Many times I have talked and written about "a path."

We often find a path through gardens, mountains, our neighborhood's and our spiritual life. But what if there is no path where we are walking? What would we do if we saw no path before us? We have an option to backtrack from where we find ourselves but backtracking is not often a good idea. Although backtracking may be helpful, I would like to suggest that you ask the Lord to show you which way He would like you to go.

Remember, when you stand in an unfamiliar place, turn to The One that knows exactly where you are and ask: "Which way Lord? Which way? Amen."

Jeremiah 29:11 NRSV

For surely I know the plans I have for you, says the LORD, plans for your welfare and not for harm, to give you a future with hope.

***

Lord, walk with me daily… that I may serve You to the best of my ability. Amen.

***

Daily communion with God is through prayer and through prayer you touch the hand that created all.

***

Have one cup of coffee (or tea) with God… For by the time you are finished miracles can happen.

Gifts Of The Spirit

I was pondering the thought of what my gifts of the Spirit might be.

I have taken classes about what my Spiritual Gifts might be, but over the years I find that some gifts come to the forefront of life when their time is in season. We do not lose our gifts given to us, but some gifts become stronger and others become lesser as the Holy Spirit chooses. When one gift seems to become lesser, it does not disappear, but finds a quiet place to rest.

All of us are blessed beyond all our expectations. Lord, let me practice the gifts that You have given me... no matter what those gifts may be. Amen.

Thanks be to God for all He has given to us. Amen.

1 Corinthians 12:4-7 NRSV
Now there are varieties of gifts, but the same Spirit; and there are varieties of services, but the same Lord; and there are varieties of activities, but it is the same God who activates all of them in everyone. To each is given the manifestation of the Spirit for the common good.

Printed in the United States
By Bookmasters